God's Creation I Am

Being Defined Only By God, Not Man

A dictionary for the created soul

Jeanette D. Haley

Dedication

To my love, my daughter, Christabel

Contents

Dedication iii

Contents v

Introduction 1

The Power of Names 3

My Daily Tracker for Redefining Myself in God 6

Worksheet #1 7

Worksheet #1.1 8

Worksheet #2 9

A portrait of you
before beginning 10

Part One 11

Part Two 78

Worksheet #3 138

Worksheet #4 139

Here is the beautiful portrait of 140

Committing or Recommitting
your life to Christ 141

I Am Already Defined Campaign 142

About the Author 143

Workshops 144

Presented To

____

From

____

Date

____

Introduction

Hᴏᴡ ᴍᴀɴʏ ᴡᴏᴍᴇɴ and young women do you know, including yourself, who can stand up and describe themselves without hesitation? How many do you know, including yourself, who can use descriptions beyond cute, strong, nice, pretty, easy going, etc. to describe themselves? How many do you know, including yourself, who believed those simple definitions are what they truly are?

It is time for us to go back to the foundation and to understand our creation. We need to understand who we are, how we were created, and the essence and substance of our being. We are not commoners. We are not like the people of this world. We are truly different and we must believe and represent that difference throughout our lives. We must redefine ourselves by God, not by man.

Pᴀʀᴛ Oɴᴇ

Part one is a compilation of scriptures that show who we indeed are in God's eyes, how He sees us, and the innate potential we have to do great and mighty things as His creation. Reading these scriptures using the word 'I' helps to increase the ability to personalize and believe this truth.

Upon reading each scripture at the bottom of the page, you have the opportunity to share your thoughts with yourself; this helps for reflection. You can go back and see the state of mind you were in at that point and time or maybe God revealed something to you as you read that scripture and you write it down to meditate on it from time to time.

In addition to scriptures, you can assess where you are before going through the redefining process of the book. Worksheets 1 and 1.1 help to begin this assessment process. You can also add a photograph to see how you looked before starting your redefining journey. Most times, what we feel and our state of being on the inside of us reflects on our face.

PART TWO

Part two covers a compilation of terms used to describe us as children of God, also, favorable descriptors that align with how God sees us are taken from the dictionary. The difference with these terms in this book is that they are not your typical descriptors used. They are so unusual but yet biblical and empowering. When we describe ourselves using these particular terms the person hearing them and the person saying them becomes uplifted and empowered.

This section also has the opportunity for you to share your thoughts for reflection.

Part Two also has a section that helps you to share how you feel going through your redefining process. You also have a place to add your photo to show how you feel and look after the redefining process.

Definitions can be memorized to describe the great creation you are.

Worksheets are a great way for you to track where you are in your life prior to reading this book and the progress you are making as you get transformed and embrace these biblical and spiritual descriptions of who you are innately. Worksheets even help you reflect on how well your prayer is evolving as you pray to God to develop relevant scriptures in your life.

SUGGESTION FOR USE:

This book can be used as a daily devotional book which allows for a daily meditative process to bring you in alignment with how you see yourself now and the true vision you have or would like to create for yourself.

Scriptures can be memorized to apply to your relevant needs and for recollection in describing who you are as a person. Scriptures can be used in prayer to God as you ask him to develop or strengthen relevant areas of need that particular scripture addresses.

This is a great tool for personal development, bible study groups, women's programs, men's programs, prison ministries, book clubs, mother-daughter bonding activities, teen identity discovery groups/workshops. Great workshop tool for women in abusive situations. Excellent husband and wife bonding activity or father and daughter or father and son bonding activity, mother and daughter or mother and son bonding activity. It's an overall empowerment tool for anyone; even men can benefit from these definitions because we're all God's Creation and these scriptures speak to creation in general.

My prayer is that, as you read this book, God's word will manifest:

"I will give you a new heart and put a new spirit in you; I will remove from you your heart of stone and give you a heart of flesh." - Ezekiel 36:26

The Power of Names

"NAME" ACCORDING TO Webster's Dictionary is a noun and means a word or combination of words by which a person, place, or thing, a body or class, or any object of thought is designated, called, or known.

"Label" according to Webster's Dictionary is a noun and is a short word or phrase descriptive of a person, group, intellectual movement, etc.

Name and label are often used interchangeably. When we label or name someone or something it represents or symbolizes the identity of that which it's attached to. Names and labels represent a curse or a blessing. Names or labels are prophecies or things to come.

When you place a name or label on something, that thing or person manifests to be the very name or label you have given it. If someone labeled you something that means a curse, go and cry out to God and denounce it, read his word and see what God has called you and rename or label yourself to mean the blessing. You may not want to change the name your parents gave you, however, you can change the names or labels that have been given to you by others regarding your character. This book has compiled some of the names God has given you to represent you being of his image and his likeness.

When God was ready to have people function in their purpose, he changed their name to represent a new identity, their new mission, his new covenant with them. God bestowed upon us some of that same power. In Genesis 2:19 God brought the beasts of the field and the birds of the air to man(Adam) to see what he would name them; and whatever the man called each living creature, that was its name. God gave man dominion and power to formulate identity. With this level of power and authority given to us by God, we have to be wise in using this authority bestowed upon us, especially when it comes to labeling others. Proverbs 18:21 "Death and life are in the power of the tongue: and they that love it shall eat the fruit thereof." Therefore, what we call or declare a thing, so shall it be.

In 1 Chronicle 4:10 "Jabez cried out to the God of Israel, "Oh, that you would bless me and enlarge my territory! Let your hand be with me, and keep me from harm so that I will be free from pain. And God granted his request." This prayer wouldn't make much sense until we read verse 9 "…. His mother had named him Jabez, saying, "I gave birth to him in pain." In short, Jabez learned the meaning of his name and didn't want that declaration spoken over his life, through his name, to be his identity, so he prayed and rebuked it and God honored and answered his prayer. This example teaches us that names and labeling can have devastating effects on the lives of people; however, it also gives hope that even if we happened to be labeled names that can curse our lives, we can cry out to God, like Jabez, and rebuke it and our God will honor and answer our prayer.

Let's take the more famous names Abraham and Sara. When God was ready to establish a new covenant with Abram and change his identity, God changed his name as a prophecy over his life. Genesis 17:5-8 "No longer will you be called Abram; your name will be Abraham, for I have made you a father of many nations. I will make you very fruitful; I will make nations of you, and kings will come from you. I will establish my covenant as an everlasting covenant between me and you and your descendants after you for the generations to come, to be your God and the God of your descendants after you. The whole land of Canaan, where you now reside as a foreigner, I will give as an everlasting possession to you and your descendants after you; and I will be their God." This is the new blessing that was about to come of his life. Genesis 17: 15-16. God also said to Abraham, "As for Sarai your wife, you are no longer to call her Sarai; her name will be Sarah. I will bless her and will surely give you a son by her. I will bless her so that she will be the mother of nations; kings of peoples will come from her." Sara's name was also changed by God to reflect the blessing that was about to come of her life. Another example among many others is Peter the disciple. Before Peter was named Peter his name was Simon. In John 1:42 "Jesus looked at him and said, " you Simon son of John.You shall be called Cephas" which means Peter. In Matthew 16:18 "And I tell you that you are Peter, and on this rock, I will build my church, and the gates of Hades will not overcome it."

From these examples, names and labels do not represent your past, they represent your future. Although people tend to label you according to your history, they are attempting to imprison your future to the past. You see, names and labels represent what is to come not what has passed. If someone calls you a negative name representative of your past, they are declaring your current and future identity being forever connected to that name or label without any change to come of it. Therefore, When you place a name or label on something, that thing manifests to be the very name you have given it.

I have a tendency to rebuke people when they say certain things to me because I am conscious of the lasting effect it can have in my life. Like Jabez, rebuke the curses in names given to you and declare the blessings that God has given to you in the names he calls you, some of those names are written in this book.

So, are you ready for a new identity? Are you ready to establish a new covenant with God? From this day forth, as you begin to read this book, do not let anyone curse you with ungodly names or labels. Rebuke and cast down any name or label that does not speak life and blessing over you.

I am a very strong advocate for anyone to get counseling from their spiritual leaders when it comes to naming their children. This type of counseling helps you to understand the meaning of names, the origin of the name you choose, and whether the name given is a curse or a blessing you're putting on your child's life and future. Ten years before my daughter was conceived I had a dream of an angel telling me the name of my daughter. I have always desired that when anyone calls her name, they are calling a blessing over her life. I knew that God didn't just give us a daughter to take up space on this earth, he sent her to fulfill his purpose. I asked God to reveal to us the name he has ordained for her, the great prophecy of her life for greatness, and he did.

I admonish you to understand this brief exhortation on the power of names and labeling and rename your self through God and see how your life changes. My in-depth study of the power of names will be out soon in my next book, The Power of Names.

When God changed people's names in the Bible, it was to improve the situation in the person's life. It was to give a new identity. It was to establish a new covenant with God. God wants to change your situation in your life, right now. Go through the book and see all the names he has given you, rename yourself and reclaim your blessings as you allow yourself to be defined Only by God, Not Man.

My Daily Tracker for Redefining Myself in God

Before I can redefine myself, I must create an unbreakable covenant with God to be defined only by Him and not by man. When we say we are allowing ourselves to be defined by God, not man, we are not dismissing that man cannot define us, we are just saying that the definitions we allow ourselves to be called by others must align with the positive, great definitions God has already given us, and not the negative definitions that make us feel defeated and hate ourselves, holding our true identity hostage.

A Covenant is a solemn agreement that you are making with God. God has never broken and will never break his promise with us. However, because he gave us the freedom of choice, we tend to go against his instructions. We are the ones that break the covenant with him by living according to the definitions and instructions of the world and not of him. He has promised to never leave us nor forsake us and to forgive us of our sins once we repent.

Repent is to change for the better; A conscious turning from evil or disobedience or sin or idolatry to the living God. **2 Kings 17:13; Isaiah 19:22; Jeremiah 3:12, 14, 22; Jonah 3:10**

Worksheet #1

Proverbs 18:21 states "The tongue can bring death or life; those who love it will reap its fruits." As we look at ourselves and think about ourselves, we must be mindful of what we are thinking and saying because our thoughts and perception of ourselves can be deadly or life giving.

Before beginning worksheet 1, spend a few minutes in prayer to ask God for his grace to help you clean up your soul to focus more on him and remove the people and things that distract you from him. Worksheet 1 will help you begin identifying in your soul the labels and people that you have to start clearing out of your life physically, emotionally, and spiritually because of the curses they have spoken over your life due to the negative labels they have attached to you. Be very raw and honest with yourself. Do not worry about feelings of shame or embarrassment.

Now that you've identified them, move over to worksheet 1.1.

Worksheet #1.1

Definitions given to you by others:

____

____

____

____

____

____

____

____

____

After completing worksheet 1.1 move over to worksheet 2.

Worksheet #2

Now that you've completed worksheet 1.1, think of how you currently define yourself and fill in below. Also, think of how you would like to be defined as. This is the vision you have and will be refining or will be creating for yourself as you develop a deeper relationship with God uncovering how extraordinary you are as his creation to fulfill his purpose.

WHAT I CURRENTLY DEFINE MYSELF AS:

____

____

____

WHAT I WOULD LIKE TO BE DEFINED AS:

____

____

____

Move on to your next step; portrait.

A portrait of you before beginning

Psalm 34:5, NLT version states "Those who look to him for help will be radiant with joy; no shadow of shame will darken their faces." Take a picture of yourself here after completing worksheets 1, 1.1, and 2. Think of this picture of being reflective of you being in a state where you've allowed yourself to be defined by man. Remember how this picture makes you feel when you look at it. Your goal will be to answer to yourself whether it inspires you, discourages you, makes you feel sad, or any of the like. After placing your picture begin Part One.

Part One

For I am God's masterpiece.

He has created me anew in Christ Jesus, so I can do the good things he planned for me long ago.

(Ephesians 2:10)

God's Creation I Am!

It is better for me to take refuge in the LORD than to trust in man.

(Psalm 118:8)

Once I give heed to instruction I will prosper, and blessed I will be once I trust in the Lord.

(Proverbs 16:20)

YOUR THOUGHTS

____

____

____

Being Defined Only By God, Not Man

God's Creation I Am!

And now these three remain: Faith, hope and love.
But the greatest of these is love.
(1 Corinthians 13:12)

I open my arms to the poor and extend my hands to the needy.

(Proverbs 31:20)

YOUR THOUGHTS

____

____

____

Being Defined Only By God, Not Man

God's Creation I Am!

For whom he did foreknew, he also did predestinate to be conformed to the image of his Son, that he might be the firstborn among many brethren. Moreover, whom he did predestinate, them he also called: and whom he called, them he also justified: and whom he justified, them also glorified. What shall we then say to these things? If God be for me, who can be against me?

(Romans 8:29-31)

YOUR THOUGHTS

____

____

____

Being Defined Only By God, Not Man

God's Creation I Am!

Before I was formed in my mother's womb He knew me, before I was born He set me apart.

(Jeremiah 1:5)

I will go; the Lord will help me speak and will teach me what to say.

(Exodus 4:12)

Your Thoughts

____

____

____

Being Defined Only By God, Not Man

God's Creation I Am!

For whoever touches me touches the apple of God's eye. He will surely raise his hand against them so that their slaves will plunder them.

(Zechariah 2:8-9)

I am confident in this: I will see the goodness of the Lord in the land of the living.

(Psalm 27:13)

YOUR THOUGHTS

____

____

____

Being Defined Only By God, Not Man

God's Creation I Am!

I will wait for the Lord; I will be strong and take heart and wait for the Lord.

(Psalm 27:14)

Praise be to the lord, for he has heard my cry for mercy. The Lord is my strength and my shield; my heart trusts in him, and I am helped. My heart leaps for joy and I will give thanks to him in song.

(Psalm 28:6-8)

YOUR THOUGHTS

____

____

____

Being Defined Only By God, Not Man

God's Creation I Am!

I will exalt you, O Lord, for you lifted me out of the depths and did not let my enemies gloat over me. O Lord I called to you for help and you healed me. O Lord, you brought me up from the grave; you spared me from going down into the pit.

(Psalm 30:1-3)

YOUR THOUGHTS

____

____

Being Defined Only By God, Not Man

God's Creation I Am!

No one will be able to stand up against me all the days of my life. As God was with Moses, so will he be with me; he will never leave me nor forsake me.

(Joshua 1:5)

I will be strong and very courageous. I will be careful to obey all the law Moses gave me; I will not turn from it to the right or to the left, that I will be successful wherever I go.

(Joshua 1:7)

YOUR THOUGHTS

____

____

____

Being Defined Only By God, Not Man

God's Creation I Am!

I will not let this Book of Law depart from my mouth; I will meditate on it day and night, so that I may be careful to do everything written in it.
Then I will be prosperous and successful.

(Joshua 1:8)

I will be strong and courageous. I will not be terrified; I will not be discouraged, for the Lord my God will be with me wherever I go.

(Joshua 1:9)

YOUR THOUGHTS

____

____

____

Being Defined Only By God, Not Man

God's Creation I Am!

I will hope in the Lord and my strength will be renewed. I will soar on wings like eagles; I will run and not grow weary, I will walk and not faint; all because I hope in the Lord.

(Isaiah 40:31)

YOUR THOUGHTS

____

____

____

Being Defined Only By God, Not Man

God's Creation I Am!

All who rage against me will surely be ashamed and disgraced; those who oppose me will be as nothing and perish. Those who wage war against me will be as nothing at all. For my Lord God takes a hold of my right hand and says, "Do not be afraid, I will help you."

(Isaiah 41:11-13)

YOUR THOUGHTS

____

____

____

Being Defined Only By God, Not Man

God's Creation I Am!

I live by faith, not by sight.

(2 Corinthians 5: 7)

I will let my conversation be always full of grace, seasoned with salt, so that I will know how to answer everyone.

(Colossians 4:6)

YOUR THOUGHTS

____

____

____

Being Defined Only By God, Not Man

God's Creation I Am!

I have been raised with Christ; I will set my heart on things above, where Christ is seated at the right hand of God.

(Colossians 3:1)

I will set my mind on things above, not on earthly things. For I have died, and my life is now hidden with Christ in God.

(Colossians 3:2-3)

YOUR THOUGHTS

____

____

____

Being Defined Only By God, Not Man

God's Creation I Am!

When Christ, who is my life, appears, then I will also appear with him in glory.

(Colossians 3:4)

Because I am God's chosen, holy and dearly loved, I will clothe myself with compassion, kindness, humility, gentleness and patience.

(Colossians 3:12)

YOUR THOUGHTS

____

____

____

Being Defined Only By God, Not Man

God's Creation I Am!

Whatever I do, I will work at it with all my heart, as working for the Lord, not for men.

(Colossians 3:23)

My ambition is to lead a quiet life, to mind my own business, and to work with my hands, so that my daily life may win the respect of outsiders and so that you will not be dependent on anybody.

(1 Thessalonians 4:11-12)

YOUR THOUGHTS

____

____

____

Being Defined Only By God, Not Man

God's Creation I Am!

I will test everything. I will hold on to the good. I will avoid every kind of evil.

(1 Thessalonians 5:21-22)

I will allow the God himself, the God of peace, to sanctify me through and through, so that my whole spirit, soul, and body be kept blameless at the coming of my Lord Jesus Christ.

(1 Thessalonians 5:23)

YOUR THOUGHTS

____

____

____

Being Defined Only By God, Not Man

God's Creation I Am!

My attitude and mind will be the same as that of Christ Jesus.

(Philippians 2:5)

I fear the Lord and serve Him faithfully with all my heart; for he has done great things for me.

(I Samuel 12:24)

Your Thoughts

____

____

____

Being Defined Only By God, Not Man

God's Creation I Am!

Greater is He who is in me than he that is in the world.

(1 John 4:4)

The Lord will supply all my needs according to his riches in glory.

(Philippians 4:19)

YOUR THOUGHTS

____

____

____

Being Defined Only By God, Not Man

God's Creation I Am!

Through me spreads everywhere the fragrance of the knowledge of Christ. For I am the aroma of Christ among those who are being saved and those who are perishing.

(2 Corinthians 2:14-16.)

I speak before God with sincerity, like men sent from God.

(2 Corinthians 2:17)

YOUR THOUGHTS

____

____

____

Being Defined Only By God, Not Man

God's Creation I Am!

I am a letter from Christ written not with ink but with the Spirit of the living God, not on tablets of stone but on tablets of human hearts.

(2 Corinthians 3:3)

My veil has been taken away because I have turned to the Lord.

(2 Corinthians 3:16)

YOUR THOUGHTS

____

____

____

Being Defined Only By God, Not Man

God's Creation I Am!

My competence comes from God; He has made me competent of a new covenant - not of the letter but of the Spirit; for the letter kills, but the Spirit gives life.

(2 Corinthians 3:6)

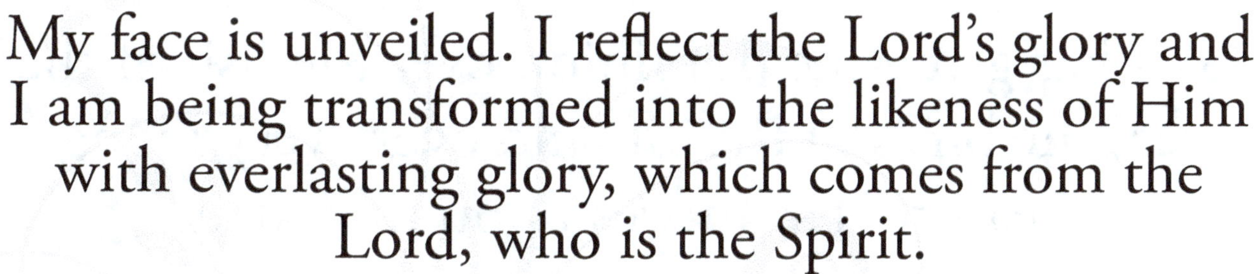

My face is unveiled. I reflect the Lord's glory and I am being transformed into the likeness of Him with everlasting glory, which comes from the Lord, who is the Spirit.

(2 Corinthians 3:17)

YOUR THOUGHTS

____

____

____

Being Defined Only By God, Not Man

God's Creation I Am!

I am hard pressed on every side, but not crushed; perplexed but not in despair; persecuted, but not abandoned; struck down, but not destroyed.

(2 Corinthians 4:8-10)

God has given me dominion over the fish of the sea, the birds of the air, and over every living creature that moves upon the earth.

(Genesis 1:28)

Your Thoughts

____

____

____

Being Defined Only By God, Not Man

God's Creation I Am!

I am a new creation, for I am in Christ; the old
has gone, the new has come!
(2 Corinthians 5:17)

I will not be yoked together with unbelievers.
(2 Corinthians 6:14)

YOUR THOUGHTS

____

____

____

Being Defined Only By God,
Not Man

God's Creation I Am!

I will not become weary in doing good, for at the proper time I will reap a harvest if I do not give up.

(Galatians 6:9-10)

Whatever I do, I will work at it with all my heart, as working for the Lord, not for men.

(Colossians 3:23)

YOUR THOUGHTS

____

____

____

Being Defined Only By God, Not Man

God's Creation I Am!

I was chosen, having been predestined according to the plan of Him who works out everything in conformity with the purpose of His will, in order that I, who was the first hope in Christ, might be for the praise of His glory.

(Ephesians 1:11)

God called me to be pure and to live a holy life.

(1 Thessalonians 4:7)

YOUR THOUGHTS

____

____

____

Being Defined Only By God, Not Man

God's Creation I Am!

I will live a purpose-driven, sanctified Life.
I stand therefore, having my loins girt about
with truth, and having on the breastplate of
righteousness: and my feet shod with the prepa-
ration of the gospel of peace; above all, taking
the shield of faith, wherewith I shall be able to
quench all the fiery darts of the wicked and take
the helmet of salvation, and the sword of the
Spirit, which is the word of God; praying always
with all prayer and supplication.
(Ephesians 6:11-18)

YOUR THOUGHTS

____

____

____

Being Defined Only By God, Not Man

God's Creation I Am!

And I know that all things God works together for my good for I love God, for I am called according to his purpose.

(Romans 8:28)

For I know that no weapon that is formed against me shall prosper; and every tongue that shall rise up against me in judgment thou shalt condemn.

(Isaiah 54:17)

YOUR THOUGHTS

____

____

____

Being Defined Only By God, Not Man

God's Creation I Am!

Blessed I am for I walketh not in the counsel of the ungodly, nor standeth in the way of sinners, not sitteth in the seat of the scornful. My delight is in the law of the Lord; and in his law I meditate day and night. I will be like a tree planted by the rivers of water, that bringeth forth in its season; my leaf will not wither; and whatsoever I touch will prosper.

(Psalm 1:1-4)

YOUR THOUGHTS

____

____

____

Being Defined Only By God, Not Man

God's Creation I Am!

The Lord is my shepherd; I shall not want.
He maketh me to lie down in green pastures;
he leadeth me beside the still waters. He
restoreth my soul; he leadeth me in the paths of
righteousness for his name's sake. Yea though I
walk through the valley of the shadow of death,
I will fear no evil; for thou art with me; thy rod
and thy staff they comfort me. Thou preparest a
table before me in the presence of mine enemies;
thou anointest my head with oil; my cup runneth
over. Surely goodness and mercy shall follow me
all the days of my life; and I will dwell in the
house of the Lord forever.

(Psalm 23:1-6)

YOUR THOUGHTS

____

____

____

Being Defined Only By God,
Not Man

God's Creation I Am!

I will love my enemies, I will bless them that curse me, I will do good to them that hate me, and pray for them which despitefully use me, and persecute me.

(Matthew 5:44)

I will not be afraid for the Lord He is my shield, my very great reward.

(Genesis 15:1)

YOUR THOUGHTS

____

____

____

Being Defined Only By God, Not Man

God's Creation I Am!

I will fully obey the Lord my God and carefully follow all his commands he gives me. The Lord God will set me above all the nations on earth. All these blessings will come upon me and accompany me when I obey the Lord my God.

(Deuteronomy 28:1-2)

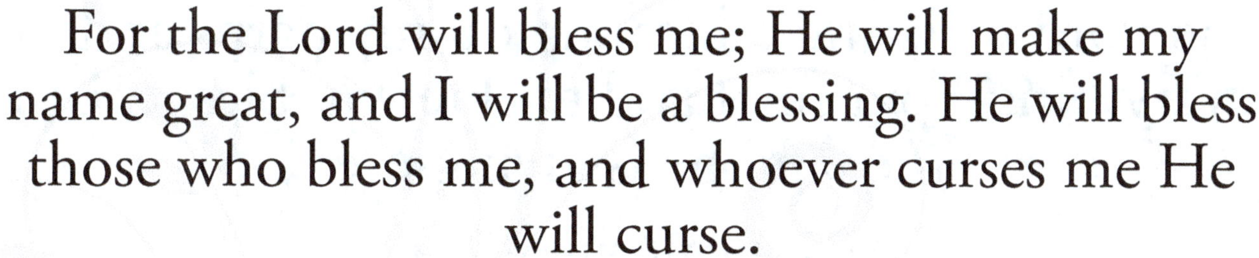

For the Lord will bless me; He will make my name great, and I will be a blessing. He will bless those who bless me, and whoever curses me He will curse.

(Genesis 12:2-3)

YOUR THOUGHTS

____

____

____

Being Defined Only By God, Not Man

God's Creation I Am!

I will be blessed in the city and blessed in the country. The fruit of my womb will be blessed, and the crops of my land…I will be blessed when I come in and blessed when I go out.

(Deuteronomy 28:3-6)

The Lord will send a blessing on my barns and on everything I put my hand to. He will bless me in the land he is giving me.

(Deuteronomy 28:8)

YOUR THOUGHTS

____

____

____

Being Defined Only By God, Not Man

God's Creation I Am!

The Lord will grant that the enemies who rise up against me will be defeated before me. They will come at me from one direction but flee from me in seven.

(Deuteronomy 28:7)

The Lord has made me the head and not the tail.

(Deuteronomy 28: 13)

Your Thoughts

____

____

____

Being Defined Only By God, Not Man

God's Creation I Am!

The Lord will establish me as a holy person, as he promised me on oath, if I keep the command- ments of the Lord my God and walk in his ways. Then all the peoples on earth will see that I am called by the name of the Lord, and they will fear me. The Lord will grant me abundant prosperity - in the fruit of my womb, the young of my livestock, and the crops of my ground.

(Deuteronomy 28:9-11)

YOUR THOUGHTS

____

____

____

Being Defined Only By God, Not Man

God's Creation I Am!

The Lord will open the heavens, the storehouse of his bounty, to send rain on my land in season and to bless all the work of my hands. I will lend to many nations, but will borrow from none.

(Deuteronomy 28:12)

I walk by faith, not by sight.

(2 Corinthians 5:7)

Your Thoughts

____

____

____

Being Defined Only By God, Not Man

God's Creation I Am!

I have been crucified with Christ and I no longer live, but Christ lives in me. The life I live in the body, I live by Faith in the Son of God, who loved me and gave himself for me.

(Galatians 2:20)

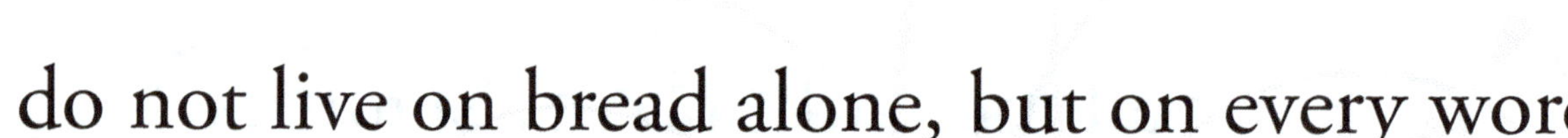

I do not live on bread alone, but on every word that comes from the mouth of God.

(Matthew 4:4)

YOUR THOUGHTS

____

____

____

Being Defined Only By God, Not Man

God's Creation I Am!

I will worship the Lord my God,
and serve him only.
(Matthew 4:10)

I am the salt of the earth.
I am the light of the world.
(Matthew 5:13)

YOUR THOUGHTS

____

____

____

Being Defined Only By God, Not Man

God's Creation I Am!

I will let my light shine before men, that they may see my good deeds and praise my Father in heaven.

(Matthew 5:16)

Because I practice and teach the commands of God I will be called great in the kingdom of heaven.

(Matthew 5:19)

YOUR THOUGHTS

____

____

____

Being Defined Only By God, Not Man

God's Creation I Am!

I will not break my oath, I will keep the oaths I have made to the Lord. My yes will be my yes and my no, no.

(Matthew 5:33 and 37)

I will love my enemies and will pray for those who persecute me. This way I represent that I am a child of my Father in heaven.

(Matthew 5:44)

YOUR THOUGHTS

____

____

____

Being Defined Only By God, Not Man

God's Creation I Am!

I will not worry about my life, what I will eat or drink; or about my body, what I will wear. For life is more important than food, and the body more important than clothes. But I will seek God's kingdom and his righteousness, and all these things will be given to me as well.

(Matthew 6:28-34)

YOUR THOUGHTS

____

____

____

Being Defined Only By God, Not Man

God's Creation I Am!

God gives me his shield of victory, and His right hand sustains me; He stoops down to make me great. He broadens the path beneath me, so that my ankles do not turn.

(Psalm 18:35-36)

I will ask and it will be given me; I will seek and I will find; I will knock and the doors will be opened to me.

(Matthew 7:7)

YOUR THOUGHTS

____

____

____

Being Defined Only By God, Not Man

God's Creation I Am!

I will go to my Lord God for I am weary and burdened, and He will give me rest. My Father's yoke is easy and His burden is light.

(Matthew 11:28-30)

I will deny myself and take up my cross and follow my Father God.

(Matthew 16:24)

YOUR THOUGHTS

____

____

____

Being Defined Only By God, Not Man

God's Creation I Am!

I will humble myself like a child and I will enter the kingdom of heaven.

(Matthew 18:8)

I call to the Lord, who is worthy of praise, and I am saved from my enemies.

(Psalm 18:3)

YOUR THOUGHTS

____

____

____

Being Defined Only By God, Not Man

God's Creation I Am!

I put my trust in you, O my God. Do not let me be put to shame, nor let my enemies triumph over me.

(Psalm 25:1-2)

I will extol the Lord at all times; his praise will always be on my lips. My soul will boast in the Lord. I sought the Lord, and he answered me; He delivered me from all my fears.

(Psalm 34:1-4)

YOUR THOUGHTS

____

____

____

Being Defined Only By God, Not Man

God's Creation I Am!

The Lord is my light and my salvation; the Lord is the stronghold of my life. When evil men advance against me to devour my flesh, when my enemies and my foes attack me, they will stumble and fall.

Though an army besiege me, my heart will not fear; though war break out against me, even then I will be confident.

(Psalm 27:1-3)

YOUR THOUGHTS

____

____

____

Being Defined Only By God, Not Man

God's Creation I Am!

I will exalt you, O Lord, for you lifted me out of the depths and did not let my enemies gloat over me. O Lord my God, I called to you for help and you healed me. O lord, you brought me up from the grave; you spared me from going down into the pit.

(Psalm 30: 1-3)

YOUR THOUGHTS

____

____

____

Being Defined Only By God, Not Man

God's Creation I Am!

I will not fret because of evil men or be envious of those who do wrong; for like the grass they will soon wither, like green plants they will soon die. I will trust in the Lord and do good; I will dwell in the land and enjoy safe pasture. I will delight in the Lord and he will give me the desires of my heart.

(Psalm 37:1-4)

YOUR THOUGHTS

____

____

____

Being Defined Only By God, Not Man

God's Creation I Am!

I waited patiently for the Lord; he turned to me and heard my cry. He lifted me out of the slimy pit; He set my feet on a rock and gave me a firm place to stand. He put a new song in my mouth, a hymn of praise to God.

(Psalm 40:1-3)

I am blessed for I make the Lord my trust. I do not look to the proud or turn to false gods.

(Psalm 40: 4)

YOUR THOUGHTS

____

____

____

Being Defined Only By God, Not Man

God's Creation I Am!

Blessed I am for I have regard for the weak. The Lord delivers me in times of trouble. The Lord will protect me and preserve my life; He will bless me in the land and not surrender me to the desire of my foes. The Lord will sustain me on my sick bed and restore me from my bed of illness.

(Psalm 41:1-3)

YOUR THOUGHTS

____

____

____

Being Defined Only By God, Not Man

God's Creation I Am!

Because through Christ Jesus the law of the Spirit of life set me free from the law of sin and death.

(Romans 8:1-2)

It is God who arms me with strength and makes my way perfect. He makes my feet like the feet of deer; he enables me to stand on the heights.

(Psalm 18:32-33)

YOUR THOUGHTS

____

____

____

Being Defined Only By God,
Not Man

God's Creation I Am!

I do not count myself to have apprehended; but one thing I do, forgetting those things which are behind and reaching forward to those things which are ahead, I press toward the goal for the prize of the upward call of God in Christ Jesus.

(Philippians 3:13-14)

YOUR THOUGHTS

____

____

____

Being Defined Only By God, Not Man

God's Creation I Am!

Whereas I do not know what will happen tomorrow. For what is my life? It is even a vapor that appears for a little time and then vanishes away.

(James 4:14)

I am radiant because I look to the Lord; my face is never covered with shame.

(Psalm 34:5)

YOUR THOUGHTS

____

____

____

Being Defined Only By God, Not Man

God's Creation I Am!

I sought the Lord, and He answered me; He delivered me from all my fears.

(Psalm 34:4)

I will be quick to listen; slow to speak and slow to become angry, to accomplish the righteous life that God desires.

(James 1:19-20)

YOUR THOUGHTS

____

____

____

Being Defined Only By God, Not Man

God's Creation I Am!

I will sing to the Lord all my life; I will sing praise
to my God as long as I live.

(Psalm 104:33)

I, like living stone, am being built into a spiritual
house to be a holy priesthood, offering spiritual
sacrifices acceptable to God through Jesus Christ.

(1 Peter 2:5.)

YOUR THOUGHTS

Being Defined Only By God,
Not Man

God's Creation I Am!

The Lord is my rock, my fortress and my deliverer; my God is my rock, in whom I take refuge. He is my shield and the horn of my salvation, my stronghold.

(Psalm 18:2)

And God is able to make all grace abound to me, so that in all things at all times, having all that I need, I will abound in every good work.

(2 Corinthians 9:8)

YOUR THOUGHTS

____

____

____

Being Defined Only By God, Not Man

God's Creation I Am!

My threshing will continue until grape harvest and grape harvest will continue until planting, and I will eat all the food I want and live in safety in my land.

(Leviticus 26:5)

YOUR THOUGHTS

____

____

____

Being Defined Only By God, Not Man

God's Creation I Am!

Then the Lord my God will make me prosperous in all the work of my hands and in the fruit of my womb, the young of my livestock, and the crops of my land. The Lord will again delight in me and make me prosperous, just as he delighted in my father.

(Deuteronomy 30:9)

YOUR THOUGHTS

____

____

____

Being Defined Only By God, Not Man

God's Creation I Am!

I delight greatly in the Lord; my soul rejoices in my God. For he has clothed me with garments of salvation and arrayed me in a robe of righteousness, as a bridegroom adorns his head like a priest, and as a bride adorns herself with her jewels.

(Isaiah 61:10)

YOUR THOUGHTS

____

____

____

Being Defined Only By God, Not Man

God's Creation I Am!

They who seek my life will be destroyed; they will go down to the depths of the earth. They will be given over to the sword and become food for jackals.

(Psalm 63:9-10)

My heart is glad and my tongue rejoices; my body also will rest secure, because God will not abandon me to the grave, nor will he let me see decay.

(Psalm 16:9-10)

YOUR THOUGHTS

____

____

____

Being Defined Only By God, Not Man

God's Creation I Am!

I watch over the affairs of my household and do not eat the bread of idleness.

(Proverbs 31:27)

The Lord has assigned me my portion and my cup; he has made my lot secure. The boundary lines have fallen for me in pleasant places; surely I have a delightful inheritance.

(Psalm 16:5-6)

YOUR THOUGHTS

____

____

____

Being Defined Only By God, Not Man

God's Creation I Am!

God has made known to me the path of life; He will fill me with joy in His presence, with eternal pleasures at His right hand.

(Psalm 16:11)

Christ Jesus came into the world to save sinners - of whom I am the worst.

(1 Timothy 1:15)

YOUR THOUGHTS

____

____

____

Being Defined Only By God, Not Man

God's Creation I Am!

When I was a child, I talked like a child, I reasoned like a child. When I became a man, I put childish ways behind me.

(1 Corinthians 13:11)

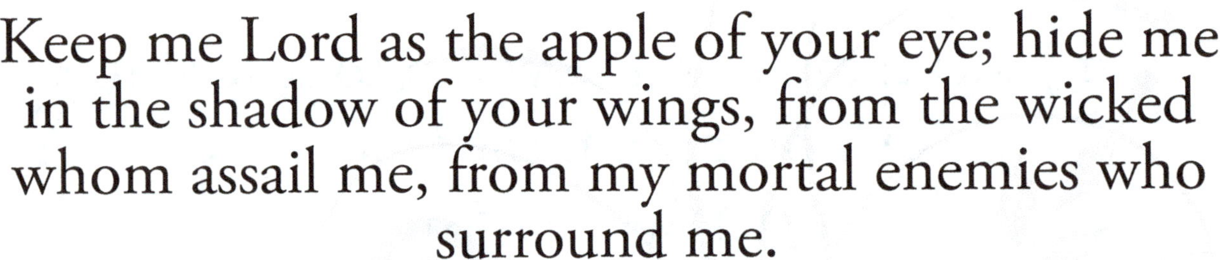

Keep me Lord as the apple of your eye; hide me in the shadow of your wings, from the wicked whom assail me, from my mortal enemies who surround me.

(Psalm 17:8-9)

YOUR THOUGHTS

____

____

____

Being Defined Only By God,
Not Man

God's Creation I Am!

I will trust in the Lord with all my heart and I will not lean on my own understanding. In all my ways I will acknowledge him, and He will direct my path.

(Proverbs 3:5-6)

YOUR THOUGHTS

____

____

____

Being Defined Only By God, Not Man

God's Creation I Am!

I have been crucified with Christ and I no longer live, but Christ lives in me. The life I live in the body, I live by faith in the Son of God, who loved me and gave himself for me.
(Galatians 2:20)

I love you, O Lord, my strength.
(Psalm 18: 1)

YOUR THOUGHTS

____

____

____

Being Defined Only By God, Not Man

God's Creation I Am!

But now thus says the Lord, he who created me, O Jacob, he who formed me, I will not fear, for He has redeemed me; He has called me by name, I am His. When I pass through the waters, He will be with me; and through the rivers, they shall not overwhelm me; when I walk through fire I shall not be burned, and the flame shall not consume me. For He is the Lord my God, the Holy One of Israel, my Savior...Because I am precious in His sight, and honored, and He loves me, He will give people in return for me, nations in exchange for my life. I will not fear, for He is with me...

(Isaiah 43:1-7)

YOUR THOUGHTS

____

____

____

Being Defined Only By God, Not Man

Part Two

God's Creation I Am!

I am Virtuous

I am a woman of worth; I am the excellence of a woman.

I am Wise

I am someone of deep understanding and skill; someone who can get desired ends with effective means; someone with sound judgment.

I am Beautiful

I apply the sound teachings of the powerful word of God to my life; as a result, the Godliness of my inner being radiates on my outer being.

YOUR THOUGHTS

____

____

____

Being Defined Only By God, Not Man

God's Creation I Am!

I am Faithful

Dependable in fulfilling responsibilities and in carrying out God's word.

I am God-Fearing

I obey the teachings of the word of God and I experience the awe and reverence in the presence of God.

I am Sanctified

I am Consecrated and set apart; I am for the use of God; I am made holy as He is holy.

YOUR THOUGHTS

____

____

____

Being Defined Only By God, Not Man

God's Creation I Am!

I am a Vessel of Honor

An instrument of God's will.

I am Obedient

I follow the commands and instructions of God.

I am Eminent

I stand out. I stand above in quality.

I am a Treasured Possession

Priceless in the sight of God.

YOUR THOUGHTS

____

____

____

Being Defined Only By God, Not Man

God's Creation I Am!

I am Loyal

I swerve not in allegiance to God.

I am a Woman of Faith

I have an unwavering trust in God. I do not walk by what I see, but by my full trust in God.

I am Devoted

I am set apart to the Lord.

I am Loved

I know and believe my creator is God in heaven and He protects, provides, and cares for me.

YOUR THOUGHTS

____

____

____

Being Defined Only By God, Not Man

God's Creation I Am!

I am Predestined

I am foreordained according to the perfect will of God.

I am Winsome

Attractive or appealing in character and appearance.

I am a Woman of Strength

I have the capacity for exertion and endurance.

I am blessed

Because I am a child of God, therefore, God will cause all things to work for my good.

YOUR THOUGHTS

____

____

Being Defined Only By God, Not Man

God's Creation I Am!

I am Consecrated

I am dedicated to the service and worship of God.

I am Gifted

My endowment comes through the grace of God.

I am Glorified

I am made glorious by bestowing admiration.

I am God's Special Possession

Chosen, taken out of darkness in to God's wonderful light.

YOUR THOUGHTS

____

____

____

Being Defined Only By God, Not Man

God's Creation I Am!

I am Unselfish

I am not seeking or concentrating on my own advantage, pleasure, or well-being. I am in consideration for God or others.

I am Intelligent

I reveal and reflect good judgment and sound thought.

I am an Inspiration

My lifestyle inspires and teaches others to place their hope and faith in God.

YOUR THOUGHTS

____

____

____

Being Defined Only By God, Not Man

God's Creation I Am!

I am Phenomenal

Extraordinary and remarkable.

I am Determined

Having made a firm decision and being resolved not to change that I am God's Creation and He is the God I will serve.

I am Remarkable

I am worthy of notice or attention. I am extraordinary, conspicuously unusual.

YOUR THOUGHTS

____

____

____

Being Defined Only By God, Not Man

God's Creation I Am!

I am a Ruler

I have dominion over the animals of the land any evil thing.

I am Chosen

I was elected by God. The Holy Spirit dwells in me to fulfill His perfect will. Therefore, I function according to the in dwelling of the Holy Spirit in me.

I am a Crown of Splendor

Because of my righteousness I am a treasured beauty to the Lord, He will designate this as my name.

I am a Royal Diadem in the open hand of God

I am a beautiful gem, treasured jewelry in the palm of God's hand.

Your Thoughts

____

____

____

Being Defined Only By God, Not Man

God's Creation I Am!

I am Forgiving

Willing and able to forgive others. I am in the habit of giving up resentment or claim of an account of an offense.

I am Dynamic

Powerful.

I am Passionate

Moved by intense emotion and strong feelings that are for and of the Lord.

YOUR THOUGHTS

____

____

____

Being Defined Only By God, Not Man

God's Creation I Am!

I am Repentant

I have turned away from evil and disobedience and sin to live for God.

I am Loving

The love I give is unconditional, Affectionate, and representative of the love of God.

I am Lovesome

Winsome, lovely.

YOUR THOUGHTS

____

____

____

Being Defined Only By God, Not Man

God's Creation I Am!

I am Hopeful

Confident. Full of hope. Shows promise and aspires to succeed in all aspirations.

I am Kind

I give pleasure or relief of good nature.
I am considerate and helpful.

I am Radiant

A light bright with joy and hope.

YOUR THOUGHTS

____

____

____

Being Defined Only By God, Not Man

God's Creation I Am!

I am Temperate

Self-restrained, not extreme in opinion.

I am Powerful

I have great power, prestige, and influence. I have great effectiveness, power and authority.

I am Sacred

Dedicated and set apart for the service and worship of God.

YOUR THOUGHTS

____

____

____

Being Defined Only By God, Not Man

God's Creation I Am!

I am Hospitable

Betokening warmth and generosity; favorable, receptive or open to new ideas.

I am Generous

Noble or forbearing spirit. Liberal in giving

I am Peaceful

A state of being from God's forgiveness. State of completeness, soundness, well-being and security.

YOUR THOUGHTS

Being Defined Only By God, Not Man

God's Creation I Am!

I am Blessed

Enjoying the bliss of heaven.

I am Self-Sacrificing

I deny myself to submit to obey the full instructions of God.

I am Affectionate

Having great love, warm regard for others.

YOUR THOUGHTS

____

____

____

Being Defined Only By God, Not Man

God's Creation I Am!

I am Admirable

Deserving the highest esteem.

I am Gracious

Pleasing, acceptable. Marked by kindness and courtesy.

I am Thoughtful

Given to heedful anticipation of the needs and wants of others.

Your Thoughts

____

____

____

Being Defined Only By God,
Not Man

God's Creation I Am!

I am Eloquent

Marked by forceful and fluent expression.

I am Strong-Willed

Having a powerful will; resolute.

I am Patient

The ability to endure under trials.

YOUR THOUGHTS

____

____

____

Being Defined Only By God, Not Man

God's Creation I Am!

I am Extraordinary

Exceptional to a very high extent.

I am Dignified

Worthy, highly honored or esteemed.

I am Sanctified

Made holy. Set apart for the use of God.

Your Thoughts

____

____

____

Being Defined Only By God, Not Man

God's Creation I Am!

I am Purposeful

Having a purpose or aim. Full of determination

I am Graceful

Displaying grace in form or action; pleasing or attractive in line, proportion, or movement.

I am Humble

Not proud or haughty, not arrogant or assertive. Freedom from pride.

YOUR THOUGHTS

____

____

____

Being Defined Only By God, Not Man

God's Creation I Am!

I am Noble

Possessing outstanding qualities.

I am Sincere

Genuine in feeling, absence of hypocrisy, feigning, or any falsifying embellishment or exaggeration.

I am Genuine

Sincerely appreciates, worships, and believes in God.

YOUR THOUGHTS

____

____

____

Being Defined Only By God, Not Man

God's Creation I Am!

I am Honest

Honorable in principles, intentions, and actions; upright and fair.

I am Peaceful

A fruit of the spirit. The presence of God within, completeness, soundness.

I'm a Reflection of God's Glory

The reflection of worth of God.

The change of my mind and body to the likeness of God.

YOUR THOUGHTS

____

____

____

Being Defined Only By God, Not Man

God's Creation I Am!

I am Joyful

A fruit of the spirit. Experiencing, causing, or showing joy. The state of being with the Holy Spirit.

I am Magnificent

Great in deed or exalted

I am Victorious

A sense of fulfillment; triumphant, pertaining to or characterized by victory.

Your Thoughts

____

____

____

Being Defined Only By God,
Not Man

God's Creation I Am!

I am Devout

Earnest, sincere devotion to duties of God

I am Meek

A fruit of the spirit. Not violent or aggressive.

I am Modest

Free from vanity, egotism, boastfulness. Having or showing regard for the decencies of behavior, speech, and dress.

YOUR THOUGHTS

____

____

____

Being Defined Only By God, Not Man

God's Creation I Am!

I am the Lamb's Bride

I'm also the church, the dwelling place of God. I am married to Christ.

I am Capable

Having power and ability to undertake tasks.

I am Pristine

Having original purity, uncorrupted or unsullied by giving one's life to Christ.

YOUR THOUGHTS

____

____

____

Being Defined Only By God, Not Man

God's Creation I Am!

I am Christ-Reliant

Having reliance or dependency on Christ.

I am Unique

Being the only one created to fulfill a specific purpose no one else can.

I am Transformed

Change in character, appearance, thinking from that of unbelievers.

YOUR THOUGHTS

____

____

____

Being Defined Only By God,
Not Man

God's Creation I Am!

I am Pure

Free from harshness or roughness. Free from what weakens or hinders the Spirit of God working in one's life.

I am a Servant of God

One who has committed their life to the service of God.

I am Fruitful

Abundantly productive, successful in all ventures. I see failures as opportunities to learn and use those lessons learned to become successful.

YOUR THOUGHTS

____

____

____

Being Defined Only By God, Not Man

God's Creation I Am!

I am **Gracious**

Generosity of spirit, kindness and courtesy.

I am **Desirable**

Having pleasing qualities, worth seeking.

I am a **Child of God**

One who believes that Jesus Christ is their Lord and Savior and apply the teachings of the Word of God to my daily life.

YOUR THOUGHTS

____

____

____

Being Defined Only By God, Not Man

God's Creation I Am!

I am Reverent

One who shows respect and/or fear for the Lord.

I am a Visionary

Having the power of visions.

I am an Organizer

One who arranges or form things into a coherent structure.

Your Thoughts

____

____

____

Being Defined Only By God, Not Man

God's Creation I Am!

I am Holy

One who is divine. Having a complete devotion to the work of God. Venerated as or as if sacred.

I am Forgiving

Does not hold wrongs against others but freely lets go of any anger or resentment towards those who have done you wrong. A person who forgives.

I am Marvelous

One who causes wonder. The highest kind of quality. Notably superior.

YOUR THOUGHTS

____

____

____

Being Defined Only By God, Not Man

God's Creation I Am!

I am a Dedicator

One devoted or dedicated to a specific cause or purpose. Service to God.

I am Free

Freedom from worldly bondage. Freedom from the dominations of the world.

I am a Peacemaker

One who makes peace.

YOUR THOUGHTS

____

____

____

Being Defined Only By God, Not Man

God's Creation I Am!

I am a Soul Winner

One who wins souls for Christ or brings souls to Christ.

I am Tender

Responding to or expressing softer emotions. I show care and consideration.

I am Christ-Like

The literal representation of the Word of God in my life.

YOUR THOUGHTS

____

____

____

Being Defined Only By God, Not Man

God's Creation I Am!

I am Brave

To face and endure hardship with courage and faith in God.

I am Diligent

Characterized by steady, earnest, and energetic application and effort.

I am Righteous

Free from guilt or sin. Morally right or justifiable.

YOUR THOUGHTS

____

____

Being Defined Only By God,
Not Man

God's Creation I Am!

I am Influential

One who possesses great influence to do good according to the word of God.

I am Ordained

To be appointed for ministerial and/or priestly duties or to the duties of the word of God.

I am Saved

Delivered from sin. Committed to living a life devoted to God.

YOUR THOUGHTS

____

____

____

Being Defined Only By God, Not Man

God's Creation I Am!

I am Christ Confident

Utter submission to the belief that God will see me through whatever circumstance there is.

I am Upright

A person marked by strong moral rectitude.

I am a Shunner of Evil

A person who deliberately shuns evil.

Your Thoughts

____

____

____

Being Defined Only By God, Not Man

God's Creation I Am!

I am Protected

One guarded and protected by the Blood of the Lamb.

I am Prosperous

Receiving the bountiful blessings, not just materialistic blessings but that of joy, peace, love, health and wellness.

I am Delivered

Freed from the bondages of sin.

YOUR THOUGHTS

____

____

____

Being Defined Only By God, Not Man

God's Creation I Am!

I am a Temple of God

I am, my body is the dwelling place of God

I am Highly Favored

I am a Royal Priesthood

Unique and set apart to win souls, pray, and reach others for Christ.

Your Thoughts

____

____

____

Being Defined Only By God, Not Man

God's Creation I Am!

I am a Receiver of Mercy

Has experienced the favor and mercy of God on their life.

I am engraved in the palm of my Father's hands

God has a tender affection and compassion for me.

I am a Letter from Christ

The Holy Spirit in me gives me the grace to worship and honor God in thought, word, and deed.

YOUR THOUGHTS

____

____

____

Being Defined Only By God, Not Man

God's Creation I Am!

I am Redeemed

It is not I that live but Christ who lives in me now that my sins have been washed away and I am covered by the blood of the lamb to keep sin from taking over me.

I am a Crown of glory and honor

I am made in the image and likeness of God.

I am the Righteousness of God

My life is surrendered in Christ for me to decrease to let him increase in me.

YOUR THOUGHTS

____

____

____

Being Defined Only By God, Not Man

God's Creation I Am!

I am the Salt of the earth

God grace and mercy enable me to live a life that reflects, preaches and radiates God's love to all no matter their fault.

I am the Workmanship of God

I am prepared to do good works which God prepared in advance for me to do.

I am Powerful

It is no longer I that live but Christ that lives in me; therefore, God will work all things for my good and I will forever remain victorious.

YOUR THOUGHTS

____

____

____

Being Defined Only By God, Not Man

God's Creation I Am!

I am a Believer

I believe in God the Father, maker of heaven and earth. Without Him, all things will not be.

I am a Praying Woman

My strength comes in knowing that my Father loves me and when I cast my yoke upon Him, He will care for me.

I am Not forgotten

God has created me for a special purpose and though I may not see my desires immediately, I know my Heavenly Father's words will not return void, but it shall accomplish that which it was sent to.

YOUR THOUGHTS

____

____

____

Being Defined Only By God, Not Man

God's Creation I Am!

I am Respectable

One who is worthy of respect. Decent in character and behavior.

I am Submissive

Obedient to the authority and principles of God

I am Considerate

Thoughtful of the rights and feelings of others.

I am Harmonious

To exist amongst others in harmony, peace, love.

YOUR THOUGHTS

____

____

____

Being Defined Only By God, Not Man

God's Creation I Am!

I am Sympathetic

Showing understanding, care, and concern for others.

I am Clear-Minded

Remaining focused and prayerful at all times and not allowing distractions to prevent you from seeking God through prayer.

I am Compassionate

Shows great concern and care for others.

YOUR THOUGHTS

____

____

____

Being Defined Only By God, Not Man

God's Creation I Am!

I am Living for the Will of God

Goal in life is to ensure everything I do is pleasing to God.

I am Overjoyed

In great delight over the blessings and sufferings God use to better you as a person.

I am Alert

Having an attitude of vigilance, readiness, attentiveness.

YOUR THOUGHTS

____

____

____

Being Defined Only By God, Not Man

God's Creation I Am!

I am Restored

Brought back into existence, reestablished, soundness.

I am Godly

Conforming to the laws and wishes of God.

I am Gentle

Using a kind, subtle, soothing approach.

YOUR THOUGHTS

____

____

____

Being Defined Only By God, Not Man

God's Creation I Am!

I am Self-Disciplined

Able to prioritize. Ability to deny oneself; knowing appropriate timing for wants and needs.

I am a Finisher

Sees every project started to its ending, does not leave anything started incomplete.

I am Justified

Because of my faith and the grace from God, I have peace with God.

Your Thoughts

____

____

____

Being Defined Only By God, Not Man

God's Creation I Am!

I am Clothed with Christ

I know I am always covered with the blood of the lamb and I wear the armor of God in my life.

I am a Sufferer

I go through the disciplinary process of God to be the best I can be in representing Him as the Holy one and Creator of everything.

I am the Likeness of God

I am created with characteristics of Jesus Christ.

YOUR THOUGHTS

____

____

____

Being Defined Only By God, Not Man

God's Creation I Am!

I am Setting My Heart on Things Above

I will inherit the Kingdom of God.

I am in Covenant with God

Honoring the instructions, plans, and surrendering to the will of God in my life.

I am Thankful

Believes that God is ruler of all things and is the reason for my existence in life.

YOUR THOUGHTS

____

____

____

Being Defined Only By God, Not Man

God's Creation I Am!

I am Truthful

True to life, speaks, and represents the truth

I am Honorable

I am worthy of being honored; entitled to honor and respect; not disposed to cheat or defraud; not deceptive or fraudulent.

I am Exemplary

Representing the greatest.

I am Estimable

Worthy of great respect.

Your Thoughts

____

____

____

Being Defined Only By God, Not Man

God's Creation I Am!

I am Astute

Accurately assess situations or people.

I am Punctilious

Showing great attention to detail or correct behavior.

I am Laudable

Receives praise and commendation

I am Discerning

Having and showing good judgment

Your Thoughts

____

____

____

Being Defined Only By God, Not Man

God's Creation I Am!

I am Distinctive

Easily distinguished from others.

I am Commendable

Deserving of praise.

I am Exuberant

Filled with great, lively energy and excitement.

I am Reflective

Thoughtful of the goodness of God in my life.

YOUR THOUGHTS

____

____

____

Being Defined Only By God, Not Man

God's Creation I Am!

I am Encouraging

Giving someone support or confidence; supportive.

I am Courageous

Very brave. Not deterred by danger or pain; brave.

I am Astounding

Surprisingly impressive or notable.

YOUR THOUGHTS

____

____

____

Being Defined Only By God, Not Man

God's Creation I Am!

I am Principled

Acting in accordance with morality and showing recognition of right and wrong.

I am Credible

Believable and convincing.

I am Deserving

Worthy of being treated in a particular way, typically of being given assistance.

Your Thoughts

____

____

____

Being Defined Only By God, Not Man

God's Creation I Am!

I am Cheerful

Noticeably happy and optimistic

I am Phenomenal

Very remarkable, extraordinary

I am Aware

Having knowledge or perception of a situation or fact.

I am Insightful

Clear or deep perception on a matter.

YOUR THOUGHTS

____

____

Being Defined Only By God, Not Man

God's Creation I Am!

I am Patient

Bearing challenges with fortitude and calm and without complaint or anger.

I am Gentle

Not severe, not rough, but gradual, moderate.

I am Perceptive

Having the power or faculty of perceiving.
Showing keenness or insight.

YOUR THOUGHTS

____

____

____

Being Defined Only By God, Not Man

God's Creation I Am!

I am Empathetic

Sensitive. Vicariously experiencing the feelings, thoughts, and experience of another of either the past or present without having the feelings, thoughts, and experience fully communicated in an objectively explicit manner

---

I am Protective

Tending to protect.

I am Intriguing

To draw or capture one's interest.

YOUR THOUGHTS

____

____

____

Being Defined Only By God, Not Man

God's Creation I Am!

I am Intelligent

Having good understanding, sound thought, good judgment.

Possessing the faculty of reasoning.

I am Graceful

Beauty of form, manner, and movement, or speech.

I am Precious

Of high price, great value, highly esteemed.

YOUR THOUGHTS

____

____

____

Being Defined Only By God, Not Man

God's Creation I Am!

I am Brilliant

Distinguished, having and showing great intelligence, talent, and quality.

I am Fair-Minded

Use of fair judgment, being impartial and unprejudiced.

I am Alluring

Very attractive, enticing.

YOUR THOUGHTS

____

____

____

Being Defined Only By God, Not Man

God's Creation I Am!

I am Breathtaking

Thrillingly beautiful, remarkable, exciting.

I am Elegant

Graceful in form and movement, tasteful, excellent

I am Exhilarating

I am able to make others cheerful or merry

I am Prepossessing

Engaging and attractive.

YOUR THOUGHTS

____

____

____

Being Defined Only By God, Not Man

God's Creation I Am!

I am **Anointed**

Empowered by the Holy Spirit for a particular work in service to God.

I am a **Crown of Glory**

I am filled with wisdom, faithfulness, and beauty. I am the receiver of God's rewards of beauty.

I am **Very Good**

Because I was created by the almighty, the all powerful, the greatest.

YOUR THOUGHTS

____

____

____

Being Defined Only By God, Not Man

Worksheet #3

Next, when you have been convicted and have turned away from the negative definitions, choose 5 descriptors from part two that appeal to you and describe how you have redefined yourself in God. Write those descriptors below.

I REDEFINE MYSELF AS:

____

____

____

____

____

____

____

____

____

____

Worksheet #4

MY NEW COVENANT WITH GOD:

Now that you have your new definitions, create a new covenant with God. Remember this scripture and how great his love is for us; Isaiah 38:17 "Behold, for peace I had great bitterness: but thou hast in love to my soul delivered it from the pit of corruption: for thou hast cast all my sins behind thy back." Therefore, let God know how grateful you are for his mercy and state your new covenant with him below. After completing your new covenant, move on to your next portrait.

____

____

____

____

____

____

____

____

Your life will never be the same, in Jesus name. Amen!

Here is the beautiful portrait of

As we learn in Psalm 34:5 "Those who look to him for help will be radiant with joy; no shadow of shame will darken their faces." Now that you have gone through this enlightening journey, this scripture is more apparent in your life. Take a picture of yourself. Reflect on your inner beauty and reassurance of God's word that you are genuinely wonderfully made and your soul truly knows that very well. This picture will be the picture that inspires and motivates you to step out in faith and pursue the purpose God created you for. If ever you become doubtful, come back and be reminded through this picture and your new covenant and your new God given definitions.

____

____

____

____

____

Committing or Recommitting your life to Christ

IF AFTER READING this book you have decided to give your life to Christ and be saved, Romans 10:9 let's you know "If you declare with your mouth, "Jesus is Lord," and believe in your heart that God raised him from the dead, you will be saved."

If you would like to re dedicate your life to Christ, pray this scripture in Psalm 51:1-19:

"Have mercy on me, O God, according to your unfailing love;
according to your great compassion, blot out my transgressions.
Wash away all my iniquity and cleanse me from my sin.For I know my transgressions, and my sin is always before me. Against you, you only, have I sinned and done what is evil in your sight; so you are right in your verdict and justified when you judge.
Surely I was sinful at birth, sinful from the time my mother conceived me.
Yet you desired faithfulness even in the womb; you taught me wisdom in that secret place.
Cleanse me with hyssop, and I will be clean;
wash me, and I will be whiter than snow. Let me hear joy and gladness;
let the bones you have crushed rejoice. Hide your face from my sins
and blot out all my iniquity. Create in me a pure heart, O God,
and renew a steadfast spirit within me. Do not cast me from your presence
or take your Holy Spirit from me. Restore to me the joy of your salvation
and grant me a willing spirit, to sustain me. Then I will teach transgressors your ways, so that sinners will turn back to you. Deliver me from the guilt of bloodshed, O God you who are God my Savior, and my tongue will sing of your righteousness. Open my lips, Lord, and my mouth will declare your praise. You do not delight in sacrifice, or I would bring it; you do not take pleasure in burnt offerings. My sacrifice, O God, is a broken spirit; a broken and contrite heart you, God, will not despise. May it please you to prosper Zion, to build up the walls of Jerusalem. Then you will delight in the sacrifices of the righteous, in burnt offerings offered whole; then bulls will be offered on your altar."

I Am Already Defined Campaign

For whom he did foreknew, he also did predestinate to be conformed to the image of his Son, that he might be the firstborn among many brethren. Moreover, whom he did predestinate, them he also called: and whom he called, them he also justified: and whom he justified, them also glorified. What shall we then say to these things? If God be for me, who can be against me? Romans 8:29-31.

When you understand verb tenses, in this case, whether it be past tense, past participle, or past progressive, you'll see that this scripture speaks of what is already done and also is about to come. For example, whom he did foreknew, whom he predestined, them he also called, whom he called, he justified, whom he justified them he glorified. This means he's already outlined everything for my existence which I am going to experience in due time. Jeremiah 29:11 says For I know the plans I have for you," declares the Lord, "plans to prosper you and not to harm you, plans to give you hope and a future." Therefore, my life is not a surprise by God, my life is well planned out from beginning to end.

This scripture gave me the conviction that whatever I desire to be, I Am Already! Because I am God's Creation and I have chosen to live according to the will of God and not my will, He has given me the desires I'm to have that are reflective of him, in my heart. The word says in Psalm 37:4 Delight yourself in the LORD; And He will give you the desires of your heart. Therefore, the more I align with God, the more I understand His will for me, the more I desire to be what he has created me to be which is already set before I was formed in my mother's womb. Therefore, all I have to do is keep seeking his face, keep living in faith, and trusting in his word and what I desire to be I Am Already, I just have to step out in faith to receive it.

Now that you have gone through this exemplary empowerment process of learning how God defines you and how beautiful and powerful you are, please join our campaign of women who have and are allowing themselves to be defined only by God, not man.

Go to
www.Godscreationiam.org/IAmAlreadyDefined

About the Author

JEANETTE D. HALEY, an Ordained Minister, Practical Empowerment Speaker, Gospel Songwriter, and Christian Playwright, was born in Georgetown, Guyana. Jeanette and her family emigrated to the United States in 1995. Jeanette earned a Bachelor of Arts degree from University of South Florida and a Master's of Science degree at Dowling College in Oakdale, New York. Jeanette's professional career encompasses positions such as Domestic Violence Victim Advocate, MultiSystemic Therapist, Community Educator, and Clinical Supervisor training skilled clinicians on how to use practical strategies to counsel children and adults diagnosed with various mental illnesses. Jeanette has since used her clinical knowledge and experience to help build up the church and better the lives of believers by creating a faith-based counseling model that targets areas such as domestic violence in the home, addressing domestic violence as a church in our modern world, substance abuse, pornography addiction, marital discord, mental illnesses, and many more.

Outside of her service, Jeanette loves spending time and traveling the world with her husband Sean and their beautiful daughter, Christabel. Jeanette and her husband co-founded God's Creation I Am! a 501(c) 3 Non profit organization established to redefine humanity according to God, not man. The organization provides life transforming workshops; trainings to equip church leaders to effectively counsel; address issues to bridge the gap between church and community; and provide world missions.

Our Workshops

I DESERVE WORKSHOP

"I Deserve" is a workshop that challenges us to keep our soul, body, and Spirit aligned to the higher good of God. We stand firmly on principle belief that we are a Spirit being and God lives in us, therefore, "I" the "Spirit" of God in me, deserves better, deserves to be treated well, and if I allow myself to be mistreated, I'm abusing God who dwells in me.

EYE VIEW WORKSHOP

Based on scriptures Numbers 13:33 "...We saw ourselves as grasshoppers, and that's how we appeared." And Luke 11:34 "The eye is the lamp of your body..."

This is a powerful workshop that challenges us to face the truth of what we see when we look at ourselves in the mirror. Teaches us how to denounce all the negative labels we've been taught or believe about ourselves and embark on a journey to redefine ourselves. This workshop unveils our eyes to see what God sees in us when we look at ourselves in the mirror.

REDEFINE YOU WORKSHOP

This workshop helps women and young women battling with the identity of their real self-worth. This workshop is unique to the other seminars because it is a three days curriculum based workshop that walks women through the process of how we end up getting lost in a negative identity and functioning. Upon completion of this workshop, participants are celebrated and celebrate their journey of discovery and the new definition of themselves in Christ. We host a graduation ceremony, make-over session, and fashion show to showcase the newly redefined, rejuvenated women.

TOOL BELT WORKSHOP

The Tool Belt workshop helps us to face the truth of the type of temple we were created to be. It helps us assess whether we are living as a sacred temple.

This workshop evaluates the kinds of tools we are currently using to determine if we're building a holy temple or using tools only fit to construct a collapsible structure.

Contact us at Jhaley@godscreationiam.org to request us to host one of our workshops at your event.

Your Thoughts

Your Thoughts

Your Thoughts

Your Thoughts